Beverley Farmer is one of our finest prose writers, but her new book, *For the Seasons: Haikus,* is likely to make her reputation as a poet too. The manuscript of *For the Seasons,* composed over twenty-five years ago, was rediscovered by the critic and scholar Lyn Jacobs after Farmer's death in 2018. The collection has never been published in full before. It joins the three prose works by Farmer Giramondo has now brought back into print: the novels *Alone* and *The Seal Woman* and the journal *A Body of Water*.

The haikus collected in *For the Seasons* are arranged in sections, beginning with spring then progressing to summer and autumn and ending with winter. One is immediately struck by the delicacy of Farmer's observations, drawn from her immersion in the coastal landscape around Point Lonsdale on the Bellarine Peninsula in southern Victoria. The constraints imposed by the haiku form encourage attention to the finest details and textures – of light and colour, of air and sand and sea – and foster an awareness of the transient life they hold, its beauty, vitality and decay. The emotion is all in the detail, the 'I' barely features, yet the mood of the seasons, and their progression is keenly registered. Farmer's poetry is remarkable in this respect, modest, self-effacing, and yet revelatory in its intensity.

Books by Beverley Farmer

Alone
Milk
Home Time
Place of Birth
A Body of Water
The Seal Woman
The House in the Light
Collected Stories
The Bone House
This Water

BEVERLEY FARMER

FOR THE SEASONS

HAIKUS

First published 2026
from the Writing and Society Research Centre
at Western Sydney University
by the Giramondo Publishing Company
PO Box 557
Willoughby NSW 2068 Australia
www.giramondopublishing.com

Cover and design by Jenny Grigg
Typesetting by Andrew Davies
in 9/15 pt Tiempos Regular

Printed and bound by Ligare Book Printers
Distributed in Australia by NewSouth Books

A catalogue record for this book is available from the
National Library of Australia.

ISBN: 978-1-923106-56-7

9 8 7 6 5 4 3 2 1

The Giramondo Publishing Company acknowledges the support of Western Sydney University in the implementation of its book publishing program.

This project has been assisted by the Commonwealth Government through Creative Australia, its arts funding and advisory body.

Contents

Introduction

Lyn Jacobs

The publication of Beverley Farmer's sequence of haikus, *For the Seasons,* is a rare gift. It is the first time her sustained meditation, in the form of three hundred and sixty-five haikus, in tribute to the days of the year and the distinctive features of its four seasons, has been published in full.

The provenance of the sequence is worth recounting. Beverley first contacted me in 1990 in response to my review of her writing in the journal *Australian Literary Studies*. A residency at Flinders University, where I was a lecturer, collaboration in a dialogue for *Southerly*'s 1998 celebration of her work, and ongoing discussions of literature, art and life contributed to a long correspondence between us and a much-valued friendship. After a short stay with her in 1999 when I checked the list of material to be included in the bibliography of my proposed study of her writing, *Against the Grain*, Beverley sent me these beautiful and accomplished haikus with the casual comment, 'these may be of interest'. I was astonished at their delicate interplay between objective and subjective response and the range and quality of the sequence as a whole. In December of that year Beverley responded to my proposal to include a chapter about her poetry with customary diffidence, advising that 'it would be wise to keep in mind that I have no standing at all as a poet, and so little to show that it's likely to seem odd giving close attention to it', and further, that 'you may have to defend such a choice, if I cannot talk you out of it'. She could not, and so in a chapter devoted to her poetry titled

'Bees in a Hive of Glass' I included everything I could find to justify my decision. When the editors returned the final draft in 2001 they commented on their increased respect for the quality of Farmer's writing, especially the poetry. In 2009 the Patrick White Award appropriately recognised Beverley's achievements.

After her death in 2018, when assisting Beverley's son Taki to gather material for the website he was creating to commemorate his mother's legacy, I discovered that he was unaware of the haiku manuscript. It was no longer on computers and after a frantic search I located my copy in an old box of research papers and postcards from Beverley's travels around the world, secured only by a rusty paper clip. I rushed to the local library to digitise it and return it to Taki's grateful stewardship.

Though Beverley sent me the sequence in 1999, I cannot confirm the timeline of its production as a record of daily events, or as the end product of a longer gestation. The individual haikus with their precise economy of expression unfold like slowed time-lapse photography recording diurnal and seasonal transformations of seascapes and landscapes, plants, birds, animals, people and objects. The closely observed changes in place and weather conditions have the immediacy and sustained concentration of a diary record. I have no doubt that if Beverley had set herself the task of writing one haiku a day she was sufficiently disciplined to do so. I know she meticulously kept notebooks (a methodology that gave rise to the powerful insights of *A Body of Water*) and that it was her custom to work and walk daily when possible. Often the colours, textures, light effects and details of sensory and sensual experience are witnessed as if seen in transit. There are variations of focus and subtle shifts in the dialectical negotiations between self and the loved locations of Point Lonsdale and Swan Bay. In a 1992 paper for a 'Women and Reading' seminar in Canberra titled 'Journeys' Beverley spoke of 'the rhythm of the stride' in language, citing Osip Mandelstam 'writing his poems in his head while walking'. Given my own experience of Beverley's exhaustive creative practice I am equally sure that scrupulous self-editing took place to achieve the coherence of design manifest in this collection.

In an email to me in December 1999 Beverley advised that 'my main reference for the Japanese forms was the introduction to *The Penguin Book of Zen Poetry* edited and translated by Lucien Stryk and Takashi Ikemoto (1981). I wish I knew Japanese. Perhaps I would never have dared though or would have deflected into the problematics of translation.' She spoke also of the aim for 'the hint of a *koan* or at least a reach for it that should be embodied in a good poem'. At Warana, in September 1998, she recalled Robert Gray speaking of 'haiku as the essence of poetry, a moment of unity with nature and as a small warm perfect-to-fondle poem – as a netsuke'. In *A Body of Water,* her interest in Buddhist tenets are evident as are influential poems and poets, among them Hopkins, Donne, Yeats, Heaney, Dylan Thomas, Robert Frost, T.S. Eliot, Plath and Dante (whose *Inferno* Farmer the linguist used to learn Italian, by comparing its French, English and Greek translations).

The sequence of haiku which composes *For the Seasons* respects Japanese traditions, acknowledging *kigo* (seasonal reference), the *kireji* (ellipsis or dash marking rhythmic divisions), and a succinct focus on the essential qualities of things (*sono mama* – to represent 'as it is'). Sharply contrasting images are juxtaposed, without expressed connection, to surprise or redirect perception. Despite the recurrence of motifs (the tideline, the cliffs, the lighthouse, the sea, sky, rockpools and selected animals and plants) there is little repetition in the charted terrain of house, garden and the local environs.

Beverley admired watercolours 'as they train the eye', and advised that 'you have to slow down and look, "narrow the aperture" as the Greek poet Seferis put it. There is much to see. It's a matter of getting it right, the shadow on the inner column of a shell, the shade of reddish brown and the mossy texture of a crab's leg.' It is a paradox that such fine scrutiny of the natural world was managed by someone whose eyesight was not good and who was customarily more comfortable using the lens of the camera as a point of access. In her poetry, intimate reflection does not negate the sense of the world getting on with its business. Beverley had a passionate capacity both to reimagine large myths and to delight in small things. I miss her intelligence, wit and wisdom. It is a solace that her insights continue to be shared through her published books.

Before her retirement in 2002, Lyn Jacobs was Associate Professor in Australian Literature and Australian Studies at Flinders University. She is the author of *Against the Grain: Beverley Farmer's Writing* (2001), the first critical survey of the author's work.

FOR THE SEASONS

For the days of spring

The lighthouse in fog:
a windmill of quiet sails
with the light in them.

One day grey and gold,
the next: beaded all over –
white, green – the plum boughs.

Tread lightly and we
will no more break the sand crust
than these gulls, these shells.

Night disembodies
a lighthouse of black stone, but
for the rolling eye.

Tails waving, two black-
birds lift off, thud breast to breast,
tumble back loudly.

A seal in the pools,
oil-skinned, humped, maned, came oozing
blindly up the beach.

An amber snakeskin
of rainwater on the fine
limbs and early buds.

Neck-deep at sea, two
black snakes, two cormorants dive
and bob up as one.

Light lies on the sea
like oil on a simmering
saucepan of water.

A blot outside, a
leap, wings, a beak as clear as
a mandarine slice.

No wind to blur bird
calls, and the cat in his morn-
ing spot of half-sun.

Tonight the lighthouse
breathes a soft damp white mist in
and out as we do.

A ball runs along
the wet sand in its own small
whirl of spindrift.

Hailstorms, sleet, salt wind –
today in the sun more plum
blossom than ever.

What was a sand pit,
storm-scoured is back to being
a living rock pool.

To watch in the dead
of night, all night, the honey-
bee dance of these stars.

A moth, but so small,
rapid, low to the sand, knife-
edged, a sea swallow.

Wave and sea snail grooves,
folds overlapped, underlapped,
from last night's high tide.

Militant grey-heads,
taller than men, the winter
ghosts of the dill weed.

Driftwood and fretty
sandstone are all dapple, grey-
brown, and veins, pits, rifts.

Most beautiful wind-
swept, the gold, red, brown and blue-
grey still naked trees.

The blossom is out,
flying in flakes on the wind.
Only not the bees.

Midway, in midair,
moon and sun past the full, poised
on the rims of dusk.

Late sun filling our
prints, the waves wiping them. A
rainbow has begun.

Brazen, the windbent
marram grass and – already –
all the lighthouse lamps.

After the chainsaws
a void as dense as the same
volume of water.

Pray for the soul of
the loquat, the gum and that
great pine, the crows' nest.

This sky is all glaze,
rumple and sheen, slick, aura
of the sunken sun.

At the flood the rock
shelf swills with water light. A
flare as a bird dives.

This room that swam in
the pine tree's green gloom – drained now,
bared to the white bone.

A shop with moon fish
for sale! Silver platters – who
was the fisherman?

The core of the stump
burned red the first time it rained,
and frothed, overflowed.

White-clad: this room in
plum-blossom light, and this, in
the death of the pine.

High in the window
pane there's a moon like a moth,
and a spider web.

Under the old pines
no sun falls, no rain – only
a dust-dry shadow.

One window still has
its light open, a lozenge
of gold, on the world.

The moon, fish-fast in
the rock pools; and now and then,
red, white, the lighthouse.

Not a lace curtain,
the moon is shining in through
the plum in blossom.

At the horizon –
afternoons of low cloud – white,
frozen, far, clear sea.

Almiríki is
rosy-flowing tamarisk,
from *almíra* – brine.

He skips on the wet
sand, hops waves, to lure us far
from his dune, his nest.

Kidskin pouch of limp
white plastic – washed bones – a frayed
strap, tail, a stingray.

Scabby grey rind, then
burnt red, then ring on blond ring,
decades, a pine life.

The loquat carted
off – the crackle of long wet
black leaves underfoot.

Wind-smoothed, these humpbacks
of sandstone, these flat shoulder
blades and rippling folds.

Inwashes, eddy
and churn and outwash of tide,
of light, of darkness.

Pier fishermen
hold taut the beaded water-
threads that bridge the gap.

Since I went away
the space has grown around my
house, the space, the light.

With no tall house next
door now, to bear the brunt, storms
have felled my old tree.

The trunk, paper, grey
yarn, knotted, and the crown all
white swarms, blossoming.

Kormós is the tree's
trunk; *kormí*, our own crimson-
lapped soft honeycomb.

The rock pools are sand
banks, sea-lettuce, sea-berry
and olive, beached at last.

Slack water, and soon
the wet sand's damascened grey
skin smoothing over.

All along the wet
sand, white-finning, the half moon:
Dry sand absorbs it.

Coral, as the seas
warm up, whitens and dies – bone,
ash, an ice garden.

Hands held high to cup
the green light of noon, the fig,
each dry branch kindling.

Swan Bay sluggish, sand-
bound at low tide, the clear light
evaporating.

Sunset, a salt haze
and gulls whose wings and red feet
drip into the bay.

My moon shadow down
there at the foot of the cliff
headfirst in rock pools.

Still air, still water,
a white night to keep the birds
awake twittering.

This hot whiff of pine
wood, how come? – drawn by the noon
sun out of the stump.

The trees in the park
are barely leafed, noon shadows
interlocked, and roots.

A grey nap, water-
gloss and then blur, this tidal
shift over sandbanks.

Kelp clumps, and black shear-
waters, wings spread all over
the gull-printed sand.

A sea breeze, a stiff
wind, as they say, stiff as green
wire, as marram grass.

Pale-skinned tea trees, white
flowers, even the rings of
cut wood shine bone white.

The branches may be
white: the trunk carves like fine-grained
rare meat soaked with blood.

Like seals they raise sleek
brown heads in the air, swaying,
deep-rooted kelp trees.

A burning glass all
day and still the ocean lags
behind in winter.

Cold wraps the swimmer
in tentacles of ripple
like a jellyfish.

More with each high tide
sprawl on the sand, mutton birds,
like the gull shadows.

Storms from the south-west
that split and felled the tea trees,
spare the green-leaved fig.

Out of this shaken
house on to a new storm-gouged,
strewn shore, boulders, wood.

Warmth at my shoulder,
the sun in cloud and loose water,
a golden being.

Pulses of wind, waves
and oil-smoothings of the wind,
hoar light on seaweed.

The sand burns. Seaweed
dying coats the hands with salt
slick much as fish do.

In wet sand, only
a spider shape, a sprawl of
weed clamping my heart.

Fox-fire, umber, black
and bone-yellow tide-thrown dry
sea wrack on fence wires.

A north wind flattens,
thins things out – trees, the light, this
heat haze, all in wilt.

Salt sheen and stillness,
the morning sea still silver
after a full moon.

Hazy water and
sky and one sound, a rock pool
fluttering, a gull.

On the tea tree tracks
shadows cross and leave shadows
engraved in hot sand.

Moon shadows, lacking
solidity, black on white,
water images.

A dense bowl of sea,
a storm brewing, shafts of rain,
sun, distillations.

Through the bay's blue-green
crust a ship's path winds, black glass;
long after the ship.

I bring garlands home,
sea fronds, sea plumes, glistening
on the garden beds.

Sea's edge to cliff was
lambent yesterday with kelp
stacks: swept clear today.

Warping in ripples
of blown sand, water, blurring,
the shadows of trees.

A night storm pending.
A glint in each pool as I
pass, opening eyes.

Rushes of rain in
the sea pools, almost over,
birds are announcing.

The book's odour of
dry leaf, ant-ridden, mottled
vanes, parched calico.

For the days of summer

The sheets I bring in
smell of heat, sun, rosemary,
white coriander.

A bat on the sand,
a tent of black wings shaking,
a shag spread to dry.

Plum flowers, plum leaves,
and the white slings blown loose, old
winter spider webs.

Rocks in the shallows
cast a sharper shadow by
moonlight than by day.

An eye in the sea
in a stone face, weed lashes,
opening, closing.

The daylight half moon.
Washed in and out of the mist,
a black-and-white bird.

Dead mouse on my spade –
wings of a moth with the sun
warm in them, soft ears.

Ropes of bull kelp and
clawed holdfasts dry in black heaps,
a hive of sand fleas.

This drenched bird has cheeks
made of lapis lazuli
and amber petals.

The stone cliff faces
stand up to their necks in lace
at full moon, high tide.

A sand garden is
the sweeps of tide and salt wind,
bare wandering threads.

Not painting the sea
again? Why? – it will only
come off in white flakes.

Dew on the long wings,
drops of white glass. A seagull
is dead in the sun.

They call and a dog
comes dolphin-diving lightly
out of the shallows.

A crab claw, red bone
and moss of brown, one white shred
and a taste of death.

White seagulls fly low
over black ones and all those
sun-struck, sea-struck rocks.

The moon and this one
tree stir, restless, thick-shadowed
over the pale sand.

Simmering and still
the sky lowers on the sea
its fire-swollen clouds.

Two or three ripples
ring the whole sea round a blue
dog wading, swimming.

Low tide, a desert,
yet from one shelf of rock fall
drops of loud water.

A fringe of water
hangs under the dog's belly
glittering, shaking.

Soon a storm will break
and the bright day be brimming
with thunder and rain.

Washed up on bottles,
goose barnacles open, wild
to breathe deep water.

The tin can we saw
rolling round in the shallows
was only the sun.

The yellow moon rose
late last night. White in the pane
it wakes me at dawn.

A limp huntsman crawls
on the sand path, pushed and pulled
by its hide of ants.

That red crab scrabbling
on the pool's rim with each wave
is dead, or a cast.

Thunderstorms and tides
pour sand in the living pools.
Each one a desert.

White knuckles and fret-
works of shell, of old china
scribbled in blue ink.

Goose barnacles massed
on a bottle at high tide
beating their dry wings.

Ripening figs, black
but hard. Lying in wait, bull
ants on the flat leaves.

The wattle birds watch
each day for the next blood-red
fig to split open.

Washed out in the rip
stay afloat. Tread water. Breathe.
Wait for the wave in.

A night of no sleep.
Said the Master once: I use
black to cool the blue.

Crests of white water
and air overhung obscure
the cliffs, the headland.

Groping in the green
dark through spans of gilded web
picking tomatoes.

The small snap of webs
finer than hair, the dry leaf
spinning the spider.

Blunt head and long spines:
a whole fish dried to leather,
only its eyes gone.

A bright turbulence
swirls up, amber in each wave,
a long cloud of sand.

The water has left
fine herringbones, nets, lumps of
jellyfish glitter.

A whiskery seed
hangs in the sun of this web
like a white spider.

A hibiscus, peach-
pale, crinkled, with the peach's
bloodstain at the core.

At midnight, no moon,
only the cross toppling and
one low star drips light.

The dark spar stretched out
at full length in the shallows
is the white lighthouse.

Windy white petals
caught on spears of marram grass:
seagull featherdown.

The hanks of weed and
the brown shadows and the sun's
interbraiding chains.

Sun-warm bodies of
water loll in the rocks and
shine like jellyfish.

Half sunk, green and scrawled
and bubbled, cold all over,
I am twice my size.

Moths pelt the lighthouse.
No, they are crickets tonight.
Already autumn.

Count them: six squid boats
on the horizon: each one
a moon on the sea.

Daybreak, a dark world.
One constellation of green
quinces is alight.

Ripening quinces
shed their blond vernix and shine
bright like yellow paint.

Flounder have one skin
that's seaweed, one that's belly
flesh, and white as rice.

Rumpled bottom sheets
of sand and sheets and quilts thrown
back, clear and blue-grey.

Spider webs hold up
the tendrils of the green vine,
its strength at the ebb.

Gulls and little terns
all huddled close at sunset
on a raft of mist.

In the heat a smell
of Greek wine: but dark, the pines,
not clear and straw-gold.

Antlers high, he breasts
the sea like a reindeer, this
dog with a big stick.

Rings of rain swell and
underneath waver spotted
fish in the rock pools.

No colour, only
monochrome washes of grey
on the sea and sky.

On calm days the nets
of light unfold and spread, crease
in the fast channels.

Drowned, a white kid glove
of breast, a penguin: blue-grey
thalidomide arms.

This orange, water-
logged, rolled on the wet sand, full
of honey, of salt.

One for a dollar,
sunflowers, and we all buy
on a wet Sunday.

A grey rain opens
holes on the pond like the round
breaths of the goldfish.

Yellow gleams, lamps on
in houses mean that now you
are out in the dark.

Beads of mercury
show where the crabs are crawling
under the lagoon.

Rosy cuttlefish
bones mark the tide's edge, and shreds,
weeds, and jellyfish.

The gull's blue shadow,
having trailed it through the pools,
perches in the sun.

After storms, fox paws
and brushes of weed wash up,
wet fur rimed with light.

White moths match the day.
Enamelled, powdered brown ones
live for the moonlight.

From the hedge at night
a warning hrrrk: the lizard,
or the wattle bird.

The insects, their buzz
and jittering, a small blaze
of the sun in trees.

An upside-down bike
without wheels is bent double
like a scared spider.

Weightlessness, this cold
clutch, this density and depth –
I'm breathing water.

Chasing the seagulls
through the shallows a dog leaves
water prints behind.

The lighthouse lantern
isn't on yet. The red glow's
just the sun setting.

The blue flower-heads,
incandescent, by lamplight
dim to lavender.

These swirls of light and
darkness are the same deep shoals
where we swam all day.

On the beach tonight
there was a cricket trilling
louder than the waves.

A heat wave, they call
this, breaking, numbing, risen
from the desert sand.

The honey flowing
from the jar! What's gold to this,
or amber? Dry stone.

Time has another
shape in the night, a bubble
that can always burst.

Dolphins break water
here, and the languid flippers
of the breathing seals.

The green seedpods, snake-
heads, of the agapanthus
have their pale tongues out.

Out of the hacked stumps
this sprawl of arms, green and red,
of the living vine.

The longest shadows
are those the moon casts over
the foot of the cliff.

At the breakwater
in a row, eight top-heavy
roomy pelicans.

The high tide is half-
way up the bluestone steps and
over the sea wall.

The melted butter
glaze on mirrors, walls, the sun
pools under the blind.

For the days of autumn

Some at blood heat, some
cold, the pools have faint waves of
sand, shadow and light.

This constant dripping
on the sand sounds like footsteps
never coming close.

Now is slack water,
dead water, between two tides,
two lives of the sea.

Clouds in the green wave
loom, chrome yellow, sand, out of
nowhere, a blank sea.

Black, vermilion, rust
red, the leaves of the green vine,
already turning.

Beacons flickering
on the far rim of the sea,
stars on the wet sand.

We are in the moon-
shade of the cliff. Now the beach
is dimmer, cooler.

Spider threads not there
by day I snap by night, stray
hairs across my face.

Inrush of the tide,
of the fractured light and wind
flattening the weed.

The rise of the tide
swamps the tepid shallows with
new cold deep water.

Now he knows the sea,
how it swallows and spews out
the beach twice a day.

Heaped high, a yellow
quilt of sand on a new grave
there in the half dark.

The grave of the bronze
boy, drowned, a *kouros*, a bronze
dolphin at his side.

The lighthouse lantern,
like a white ball bounced up and
down in a rock pool.

A clear sky, full moon,
stars, all reflected in rain
pools black as shadow.

The louder the hail
of apples on the tin roof,
the stronger the wind.

At midnight, a moon
so full that a bird waking
starts its chittering.

Not the red of death
but life blood in the gumtips,
a ripple of fire.

In the tea tree shade,
hollow boughs, dry leaves and sand
and a grey silence.

Grey, sullen, the sea
with the sun gone out of it
could be any depth.

A pomegranate
sun, a honeydew melon
moon in the balance.

You feel it at once
as sharp as a cool change, this
return of the tide.

Swan songs of summer,
coda, cadenza, pale days
of hot sky and sea.

Milk one last black drop
from the fountain pen, sea blood
on dry cuttlebone.

Russet, we wallow
through late sunshine and the path
of the daylight moon.

We are slippery
wet and red-gold from the thighs
up, moonlight below.

I go to pick figs
and lacewing moths off the boughs
alight on my arms.

Figs soft in my hands
and more up high, swelling, bruised.
Milk stains on my shirt.

No rain these two weeks
of the waxing moon. Dew is
dripping from the eaves.

A mist-laden sky
but, low and cold, a sharp wind
scouring the green sea.

Silky upswillings
and backsurges, sand and cool
water on bare feet.

The green tomatoes
take only hours to be red
gold balls of warm seed.

Fewer brown-dappled
yellow fig leaves by the day,
as the figs darken.

A flight of shadows
whirling, dazing us, black here
and white overhead.

A black trunk lying:
long teats in a row, sunlit
toffee, soft amber.

A shaft of blood sunk
through shoal and sandbank, driven
down by a red sun.

In this world without
colours, the water is depth
or transparency.

Coming in after
a moonlight walk, spider webs
caught in my lashes.

Placid afternoons,
the pier wading kneedeep,
petticoat hanging.

The breath of the earth,
dusty, tawny at sunset,
burning, an oast-house.

Whatever is smeared,
slicked, sodden with wet glistens
with gold lacquer. Red.

Strung over sandstone
crevices, a grey fabric,
spiders and bronze flies.

A line of poplars
against the late sun, burnt brown
as tobacco leaves.

They talk of harvest
moons. Here we have harvest suns,
long flows of honey.

Those are hills over
the sea, the white shag of mist,
or blue-grey cloud banks.

The small waves crinkle,
narrow as a squid's mantle,
soundless on the sand.

The waves at twilight,
their crimped edge, like quince jelly
setting on a plate.

These pools have beaches,
curved ridges of sand and rock
etched black with mussels.

The dog by the pool's
edge shakes and sends spray flying,
clots, opacities.

All the sea's noises
are clear and close as if this
bed were in the sand.

When the waves peel back,
pores in the sand blow domes of
bubble on bubble.

Swimmers enfolding
fawn, grey-green and lemony
pallors of storm light.

Pillars of dark cloud
in sky and sea, and out west,
toppling walls of storm.

The night of faint rain,
cricket trill, snails, lighted ships
smooth on the water.

Not burrs, bees, brown husks
crouched in the dusty gold spines
of the banksias.

One great hot salt breath
has flattened the whole bay, those
slow wet greenish swathes.

By the look of things
wind is the stronger, hurling,
winnowing the sea.

A blaze of white fire
in waves and printed sand, on
the bent marram grass.

No red fig grains here –
ash, excrement, uncurling
and blind, a pale grub.

Ice-crusted, the night,
and halfway down the jetty –
heat, salt, the soft wind.

Bursting its river-
skin in bright air, how does it
know, the dragonfly?

Ceaseless, steadfast, skip-
ping the waves like a pebble,
a lone cormorant.

Drifts of wind wrinkle
the fan of the rock pool, pull-
ing it smooth again.

The wave line forwards
is foam, backwards is folds, frills,
gathers of shadows.

All, whether spindrift,
surf, foam, spume or mass of cloud
or wing stir – all, white.

A wavering beam
tonight, a flounderer's torch
on the still surface.

The lighthouse lantern
keeps thrusting on walls of mist
its cage of shadow.

At the cave mouth, bright,
soft, a fall of drips, and pits
and rings in dry sand.

Where there is no sun
it could be water or air
in the grey rock pools.

Bands of shine winding,
cloud, sky, of almost-mirror,
all down the wet sand.

A bawling south wind.
The ferry is an iceberg
on the horizon.

Lowslung, grey, with slit
white eyes, a puffy white mouth,
sand-caked – a whole shark.

Lights on the bay break
off from the town's mosaic
of lights to drift close.

Scratch scratch at my head.
The rat in the wall boards (tongue-
in-groove) is awake.

Daytime sadness of
lights left on in small windows
all along the street.

A whole day of rain.
Only the tide-washed sand is
smooth and tight as skin.

Sure-footed he steps
from pool to pool, paddling and
trailing water strings.

Ringed beads of last night's
rain flare on grass blades and swell
the pale grain of them.

Lichen flowers in
rainy sea colours on dry
branches, whiskery.

The swamp is living
skin, a shadow of water
twitching, shivering.

In the deep water-
fall pool, milky, cold, the rocks
feel as warm as flesh.

The filling moon, and
again we sleep light, wake light
in frog song, bird song.

My shadow at sun-
set on the long grass, a green
pyramid in gold.

Trails of river shine
where a boat passed or a wind's
dank saltwater breath.

The moon is water
on palm fronds; and crazed ice, hung
high in a pine crown.

Strung still on the glass
door where the lamplight hid it,
headlong, the spider.

The pool, the lotus –
no, it's a high bamboo husk
mirrored, and the sun.

Wild, the white fig, dark.
For roots it has hands that cling
in air to the bole.

Charcoal scratches on
moonlight, the long tassels, sea-
washed, of the she-oak.

The birds are awake.
(This bright moon.) Blurred shadows go
stitching my clear one.

Stingrays in one mass,
one overlapped swift moon shape,
in fear of the shark.

Noon, and the shadows
fly low: sharp on the sand, they
fade out in the sea.

For the days of winter

Gold flecks on the lake.
Some are high clouds, some lamps, some
birds caught in between.

A house made to keep
out the midsummer sun with
walls of naked boughs.

Breath of the soil, leaf
mould, water, incense, rising
with the evening star.

Shadow is alive,
newborn of the sun, asleep
under the still trees.

Steady wingbeats of
the rowboats homing. Dark trees
mirror the river.

This grass has a pearl
sheen of dew like the opaque
swift flank of a fish.

No moon, just the stars
on the white sand, the milky
way, the sea's loose edge.

Like hands, the last brown
fig leaves as they curl up cold
fingers in the rain.

While I was away
the apples fell with no trace,
all gone to grey earth.

Do the red leaves stay
alive as long as they cling
on, veins filled with sun?

These days the sun breaks
through the low mist around noon
as if through deep water.

The spider cringing
under the ledge can’t see what
a shadow it casts.

Midwinter, noon. All
the lagoon gapes at the webs
of one pelican.

Once a dark fig falls
it is hard to find among
these ripe wet soft leaves.

Purple irises,
white tulips and candles burn
in a dead friend's house.

At her open door
a posy of violets,
water prints, red leaves.

Sly wind-creaks and shifts
through the trees, like the passage
of loose animals.

Swans at the lagoon
verge drift with their black heads high
and studded with drops.

Whale time, when this sea
may bring forth a great wonder
of hot breath, hot blood.

Grey streaks and smudges
falling at the sky's rim: here,
at the centre, dry.

A glow in the west
by five, like lamplight, like fire
in a curtained room.

The longest night, clear
moon and a high wind singing
in the cold lighthouse.

Autumn shrouded all
the windows and eaves with white
webs, empty, greying.

A roaring ahead
as we climb the dune over –
white, bare – a furnace.

Some days these rooms are
brimful of tree-filtered sun,
watery dadoes.

Leaves at the pane, so
plumped up with rain that they float
and flare like glass beads.

A lean cormorant
on one rail, wings draped, and gulls,
stout, still, opposite.

Weeds of worked bronze, gold,
amber, aflame, deep-shadowed
as if by a lamp.

Cloudy, smudged with blue
all afternoon the moon hung
full on the lighthouse.

Grey bones in the wind,
the wavering fig, one leaf
at the crown lifted.

Midnight after rain:
the moon has a ring of mist
in a ring of fire.

Shrivelled vine tendrils
and leaves in crimson scrolls that
enshroud the spider.

Sunrise, russet light
in the bare apple boughs, their
skin of rainwater.

Tassels of seaweed
and water string out in long
fringes from the rocks.

Never in summer
is the sea so clear, green, gold
and blue at such depths.

Champagne glasses on
the rock shelf, wedding pictures
in a veil of spray.

Lying clenched under
the fig are a hundred soft
wet dark brown suede gloves.

Across the water-
bitten cliff face at sundown,
shuttles of swallows.

Dark-etched beneath us
the rocks and sand and tall weed
warp, dilate and shrink.

Marram grass, sword grass,
wheaten sprays, then the thin skins
of the sea below.

A wagtail paces
me down the beach under these
cliffs, fanning himself.

Low water, quiet
at noon, and quiet boats in-
shore, fish or no fish.

No glass as fine as
this pane, sky-mirroring, laid
between sea and sand.

Shadow alone is
solid in this rock pool's rap-
id fume of ripple.

The battlements and
grey caves? All buried in this
avalanche of sand.

Yellow as a sponge,
this beach, all dog-claw prints and
open breathing holes.

Black trunks and branches
lie on the grass below in
perfect effigy.

Low in the bare black
crowns of the tea trees the sun
burns like a bushfire.

The consistency
of sliced fish, raw, marbled, light
pink, in the wet sand.

The sun like a log
fire goes out leaving darkness
and this ashen frost.

If on a clear day
there are humpback whales, singing
comes up from the sea.

Huddled like bull seals
in the shade of the sea wall,
streaming, the brown kelp.

I gather dead weed,
torn holdfasts stiff in the air
like a swimmer's hand.

A glint on the rain
and on the one long wave up-
heaving the bay lights.

High tide, surf, spray and
fog flooding the western dunes,
embers on the crests.

The full moon rose hot
as sunset out of a sea
of stars and beacons.

A still night, and now
the spider web is frozen
onto the thin pane.

Midwinter summer,
a wind out of the desert
hatching flies, and buds.

The tea trees hold on
to dead boughs, aslant, like rain,
visible through leaves.

The gold light that burns
through the tree prints its shape on
the gold wood of walls.

Fan lines of faint rain
on the yellow horizon
over the lagoon.

Waves of clear amber
each with a black underlip
vanish in the sand.

Trees of copper wire,
the trunks and roots iron-dark
as if in water.

Early afternoons,
cliff shade down to the sea's edge
and all the sand cold.

The tree tops reach back
into another time zone
where it's still full day.

The salt winds have stripped
these trees back to tufts like nests
and a bird or two.

The new leaves must push
their way through the golden pelt
of the old lichen.

So few cobwebs. Now
and then a shimmer, a hair,
filaments of light.

The last of the light –
the clouds browning like leaves – and
the first, the new moon.

A meander of
red light, the edge of the sea,
veiled, unveiled and veiled.

Midnight, long after
moonset, the lighthouse beam lost
in the Milky Way.

After rain the fig
tree dangles a jewel from
every elbow.

There are pits, caves, noon-
struck hollows of darkness carved
in the sandstone cliffs.

Rain, then stars, a half
moon flat on its back, and light
underfoot, water.

People and dogs out
early all have the same white
thought balloon (It's cold).

Even the noon sun
lies low, slant, barely kindled,
an apparition.

Who would imagine
the grey fig, naked, bone-dry,
harboured abundance?

Winter light, like low
firelight, like rain, burnishes
surfaces in depth.

I pull down the webs
in the time of ease between
old spider and new.

Two pincers, dull red,
torn away, still heavy with
meat: no further trace.

We were wet with spray
and bathed in yellow along
the darkening strand.

A sun no brighter
than the moon. Seabirds fly out
of the cloud, the wind.

Overprinted on
the dry sand, creases, torn spills
of froth and wave scrawls.

The island snowbound,
the southerly full of ice,
the long waves of snow.

A second nightfall,
thick, sudden, as loose as smoke,
clouds over the moon.

Why a tall wire fence
at the foot of the dunes? It
keeps the sea at bay.

A white umbrella
spreads, folds, spreads ribs of shadow,
its pole the lighthouse.

Red japonica
and the yellow wattle, fire-
flowering at dusk.

Kelp tossed overnight
headlong over the sea wall,
red-brown bog tresses.

Crimson-beaked, tall black
lilies outspread, swans in the
still of the low tide.

A dog in the white
shallows of the moonlight swims
and snatches a stick.

Trees of kelp rise and
spread boughs and fall all in the
green air of one wave.

Celebrating Thirty Years

The Giramondo Publishing Company is an independent, Australian, university-based literary publisher of award-winning poetry, fiction and non-fiction, renowned for the quality of its writing, editing and book design. Founded in 1996, it has made a singular contribution to Australian literature for the past thirty years. Visit our website to find out more about our new releases, our literary magazine HEAT, and our classic titles. https://giramondopublishing.com/

About the author

Beverley Farmer (1941–2018) was the author of four collections of short stories, including *Milk*, which won the 1984 NSW Premier's Award for Fiction; the novels *Alone* (1980), *The Seal Woman* (1992) and *The House in the Light*, which was shortlisted for the 1996 Miles Franklin Literary Award; and the writer's notebook, *A Body of Water* (1990). *The Bone House*, a collection of essays on the life of the body and the life of the mind, was published by Giramondo in 2005 and *This Water: Five Tales* in 2017: it was longlisted for the Stella Prize. Since then Giramondo has republished *Alone, A Body of Water* and *The Seal Woman*. Writing across many different genres, poetry as well as prose, Farmer is considered one of Australia's most important authors.